CELEBRATING THE PEOPLES AND • CIVILIZATIONS OF AFRICA™ •

THE

YORUBA

OF WEST AFRICA

Jamie Hetfield

The Rosen Publishing Group's
PowerKids Press™
New York

Published in 1996 by The Rosen Publishing Group, Inc.
29 East 21st Street, New York, NY 10010

First Edition

Book Design: Kim Sonsky

Photo Credits: Cover and p. 8 © Eliot Elisofon/Eliot Elisofon Photographic Archives, National Museum of African Art, Smithsonian Institution; p. 4 © Herbert M. Cole; pp. 7, 11, 15 © C. M. Hardt/Gamma Liaison; pp. 12, 16, 19 © Phyllis Galembo/Swanstock; p. 20 © Brian Palmer/Impact Visuals.

Hetfield, Jamie.
    The Yoruba of West Africa / Jamie Hetfield.
        p.   cm. — (Celebrating the peoples and civilizations of Africa)
    Includes index.
    ISBN 0-8239-2332-0
    1. Yoruba (African people)—History—Juvenile literature. 2. Yoruba (African peoples)—Social life and customs—Juvenile literature. I. Title. II. Series.
    DT474.6.Y67H47 1996
    966'.0049633—dc20
                                                                                        96-6993
                                                                                          CIP
                                                                                          AC

Manufactured in the United States of America

CONTENTS

WHO ARE THE YORUBA?

The **Yoruba** (YOR-oo-buh) are one of the best-known peoples of Africa. Their beautiful art and their religion are known all over the world.

The Yoruba believe that God has many lesser gods and goddesses to help him. Shango is the God of Thunder and his symbol is lightning. Olokun is the Goddess of the Sea. There are also many others. The Yoruba make special art for each god or goddess. They have many holidays and festivals for them.

◀ Yoruba traditions are known and respected all over the world.

WHERE DO THE YORUBA LIVE?

Most Yoruba live in Nigeria and Benin, two countries on the coast of West Africa. The Yoruba are known for being **urban** (ER-bun). That means that they live mostly in cities, towns, and villages. The three largest cities in Nigeria are in the area where the Yoruba live, Yorubaland.

Yoruba towns usually have a busy market in the center. Many Yoruba women are traders and run stores there.

Everything from food to beautiful ▶
cloth is sold at Yoruba markets.

YORUBA MEALS

Many Yoruba have farms near their homes. The Yoruba grow many crops. One important crop is cocoa, which is used to make chocolate. They sell the cocoa to people all over the world.

The Yoruba eat many different foods, including rice, yams, and **cassava** (kuh-SAH-vuh). They also raise animals and hunt wild birds and animals. The Yoruba who live near the ocean eat fish and shrimp.

◀ This family is preparing cocoa beans grown on their farm.

YORUBA HOUSES

Each Yoruba house is built with a square area in the center called a **courtyard** (KORT-yard). The courtyard has no roof so lots of sun shines in. This is where the family meets and spends time together. During the dry season, when it doesn't rain, Yoruba children sleep outside in the courtyard.

Each Yoruba house overlooks a courtyard. ▶

YORUBA KINGS

In the past, there were many kingdoms in Yorubaland. Most kingdoms had their own kings. It was believed that kings were very powerful and that their power was hot. For that reason, kings couldn't let their feet touch the ground. If they did, the Yoruba believed, the soil would be burned and crops wouldn't grow. So Yoruba kings wore sandals.

The Yoruba also believed that a king's gaze was powerful. Most kings wore beaded veils to cover their faces and eyes so their people wouldn't be harmed by their gaze.

◀ Even today, Yoruba kings are believed to be very powerful.

NAMING OF CHILDREN

The naming of children is very important to the Yoruba. A child is usually named after one of his or her **ancestors** (AN-ses-terz).

Usually a baby and his or her parents wear their best clothes for the naming **ceremony** (SEHR-uh-moh-nee). The oldest woman from their part of town is chosen to help. She puts a little honey, red oil, salt, fish, and onion in the baby's mouth. Then the woman tells everyone what the name of the child will be.

Yoruba children are usually named after their ancestors. ▶

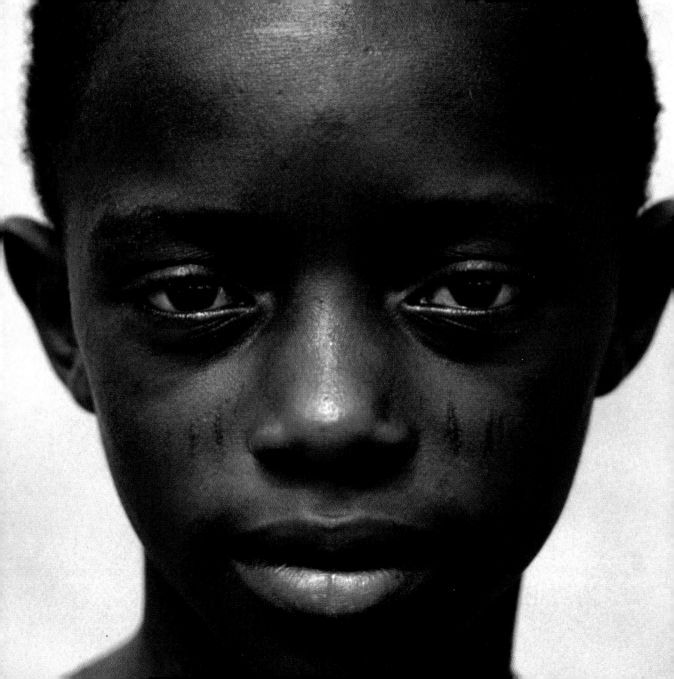

TWINS

The Yoruba have more twins than any other group of people in the world. They believe that twins are godlike and that they bring good luck to the family. They also believe that all twins are in a hurry to get to heaven. Parents of twins are afraid that the twins may die young in order to get there. To keep them on earth, parents carve a little sculpture called an ***ibeji*** (ee-BEH-jee). They clothe and decorate it, and leave offerings of food for the *ibeji* as a way of persuading the twins to stay alive and on earth.

◀ Parents of Yoruba twins may keep the *ibeji* in a special place called a shrine.

17

RELIGION

The Yoruba believe everything in the universe is filled with a spirit called **ase** (AH-shay). This life force is found in all kinds of things like people, animals, rocks, and even songs. It can be good or bad, just like the gods of the Yoruba.

When it becomes hard for a Yoruba person to understand the gods or the world around him, he asks for advice from a priest called a **babalawo** (bob-a-LAH-woe). The *babalawo* is a link between the gods and the Yoruba.

The *babalawo* knows all the holy Yoruba songs and prayers by heart. ▶

FROM AFRICA TO THE AMERICAS

Many Yoruba came to North and South America as **slaves** (SLAYVZ) more than 150 years ago. But they never forgot their home in Africa. Those Yoruba carried their culture with them, including their religion, language, music, dance, and **cuisine** (kwiz-ZEEN).

Many people in North and South America now follow some of the Yoruba ways.

◀ You can see many African traditions in celebrations, such as this one held in New York City.

YORUBA ART

Hundreds of years ago the Yoruba made beautiful **sculptures** (SKULP-cherz) out of metal and stone. Today, the Yoruba make sculptures out of wood. They also create beautiful beadwork and costumes. Yoruba art can be seen in museums and at big festivals and parades in different places around the world.

In the United States, many parades and celebrations feature Yoruba costumes.

22

GLOSSARY

ancestors (AN-ses-terz) The relatives who came before you.

ase (AH-shay) Life force or spirit.

babalawo (bob-a-LAH-woe) Priest.

cassava (kuh-SAH-vuh) Starchy vegetable used to make special breads and other food.

ceremony (SEHR-uh-moh-nee) Set of acts performed on a special occasion.

courtyard (KORT-yard) Closed-off open area in the middle of a building.

cuisine (kwiz-ZEEN) Food and style of cooking from a particular culture.

ibeji (ee-BEH-jee) Small wooden statue carved to represent twins.

sculpture (SKULP-cher) Art of making forms representing people or objects.

slave (SLAYV) Person who is owned by someone else.

urban (ER-bun) Having to do with towns or cities.

Yoruba (YOR-oo-buh) A people who live in West Africa.

INDEX